GOD VS PEER PRESSURE

A TEEN'S

SURVIVAL GUIDE

TKO!
I'VE GOT THE
POWER!

PENELOPE A. FIELDS

Topaz Publishing

READING ENTERTAINMENT
FOR THE ENTIRE FAMILY

Copyright© October 2013 Penelope A. Fields

Cover Art: Dawne Dominque Copyright October 2013

Illustrations: Dreamstime

Editor: Kase Reed, Topaz Publishing

Line Editor: Arianna Alexander, Topaz Publishing

ISBN-10: 0615898262

ISBN-13 9780615898261

Genre: Juvenile, Teens & Young Adults

Topaz Publishing, LLC USA

www.topazpublishingllc.com

DEDICATION

God VS Peer Pressure

A Teen's Survival Guide
Volume One

To all parents who are at their wits end.

Peer Pressure is a constant threat to your teen. It is a force more powerful than you could ever imagine. Many times, your teen is confused by what they hear and see, yet they are eager to fit in. Empower your teen with the word of God. Help them understand God's plan for their life.

CONTENTS

God VS Peer Pressure

A Teen's Survival Guide

Every teen needs: God's Survival Guide

Being a good parent is very difficult. Each day, your teen is faced with difficulties you could only once imagine. In the Survival Guide, God VS Peer Pressure, Ryder and Madison are faced with some hard decisions about sex. As your teen reads about their experiences, they will relate to these powerful forces.

After identifying with these two typical teens, the Survival Guide will clear up the confusion. Your youth will learn what God has to say about sex and their bodies. Peer Pressure is strong, but God is stronger. Empower your teen. Help them understand God's plan for their life.

CHAPTER ONE

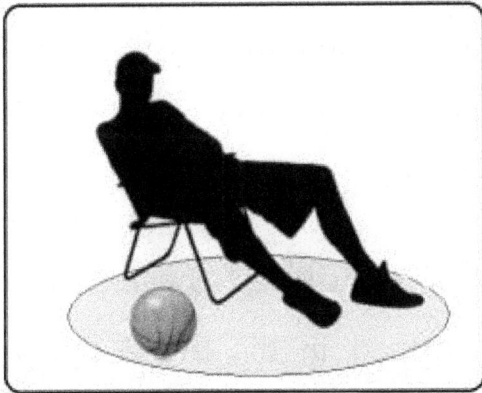

Ryder's Story

With ear buds tucked inside her ears, Madison sat on the patio and nodded her head to the rhythm of her music. In an adjacent backyard, two young men played a friendly game of basketball. Humming softly to herself, she seemed unaware of the bustling activity across the fence.

Ryder was a senior in high school, while Corric attended a local college. Since Madison and Ryder attended the same church, they often walked to services together.

Corric dribbled the ball. Suddenly, he stopped in his tracks. He took an obvious stare at Madison, and then wiped his hand across his lips. "Who's that?"

In Corric's silence, Ryder retrieved the ball. Taking advantage of his friend's preoccupation, he tossed it at the goal. It circled the rim a few times then fell through. When Ryder glanced at Corric, he appeared confused. "Who?"

The ball bounced once before Corric caught it. "Her." He pointed to Madison.

"Oh, her." Ryder nodded. "That's Matty, my neighbor." Instantly, Ryder slapped the ball from Corric's hand, and then dribbled it on the pavement.

"Have you hit that?"

"Hit what?" Ryder asked, as he danced about.

"You know. That hot babe on the patio."

"What hot babe?" Glaring at Corric, Ryder scowled. "What are you talking about? Matty. Man, she's no match for you. She's just an innocent kid."

Corric pulled his cap sideways, and then walked toward the fence. He drew Matty's attention, and then winked at her. "Girl, yes. Little, no. Besides. I like 'em young and stupid." He tilted his chin toward her. "Introduce us."

Grabbing Corric's wrist, Ryder restrained him. "Come on, man. I know your rep. You can't go there. Not with her. I've known Matty for years — goes to my church. She's a decent girl."

Fists curled, Corric jerked his hand free. "I like decent girls. They're naive and easy. They believe babies come from storks. Besides, she doesn't fill out those shorts like a kid."

Ryder placed his hand on Corric's shoulder. "Come on, dude. Think. That's jail bait."

"What is she, thirteen, or fourteen? And, I don't need any of your righteous God babble. Besides, she can make up her own mind. With a little help." Again, he walked toward the fence.

Feeling anger rise in chest, Ryder slammed the basketball into Corric's back. Corric winced in response. "I'm warning you, man. If you go anywhere near her, it's on. It's me and you, man."

Initially, Corric stumbled. When he regained his balance, he turned. "I can't believe you'd hit me because of some snot nose kid."

Gnashing his teeth, Ryder rushed Corric and punched him in the jaw. The blow knocked him to the ground. Staggering to his feet, Corric wiped blood from his mouth and then charged for Ryder's stomach. With both fists clenched, Ryder pounded the back of Corric's neck, then tossed him to the ground.

At that moment, Pastor Frederick, who had been visiting Ryder's home, burst through the back door. He sprinted into the backyard. When Corric insisted he'd have his revenge, the pastor pulled the young men apart. Then, Pastor Fredrick held his hands to their heaving chests. "What's going on out here? Who started this?"

After Ryder explained what happened, Pastor Frederick turned to face Corric. "Corric. You are much older. You should have known better. This is a form of disrespect that will not be tolerated. Just like you, Madison is a child of God. God did not create her just to satisfy the lust of *your* flesh." The pastor folded his arms. "What if she were your sister?"

Eyes narrowed, Corric picked up his cap, dusted it off, and frowned. "I don't have any sisters. If I did, it would be her business who she slept with; not mine."

Pastor Frederick shook his head. "Don't you see? It doesn't matter who the young lady is. A man respects a lady, merely because she *is* a lady."

Leaving the Pastor's presence, Corric stormed toward the gate. After he placed his hand on the latch, he turned and stared at Madison. "I still say; if I ever catch her alone, she's mine."

"You are as heartless as Satan," the pastor yelled. "Get out of this yard. If I see you anywhere near Matty, the police will take care of you."

"Humph. Is that all, old man?" Corric swaggered through the gate, leaving it ajar. "Who's scared of these toy cops."

Although Pastor Frederick contained his anger, his face reddened. He walked to the gate and watched Corric get into his car. After Corric drove away, he closed the gate and turned to face Ryder. "You don't settle things by fighting. However, in this case, you were trying to protect an innocent girl."

Together, they walked to the house. With his arm on Ryder's shoulder, Pastor Frederick opened the door. "Corric doesn't respect himself, so we can't expect him to respect others. He will learn his lessons hard. However, you're right. We must protect Madison."

~End~

CHAPTER TWO

Madison's Story

From the garage, fourteen year old Madison strolled through the kitchen door. The delicious aroma of garlic bread permeated the room. "Yay. Lasagna and garlic bread."

Hannah, her grandmother, stood at the sink washing dishes. "Yes. I recalled someone throwing some strong hints yesterday."

"Thanks." Matty removed her ear buds, and then lowered her backpack to the table. "Mom never cooks homemade lasagna, and she's always gone."

"Matty. Your mom is a single parent. She works two jobs to make ends meet. Cooking a meal is the least I can do to help out. Plus, this family should eat together more often. Don't put your backpack on the table, dear. A table is for eating."

Madison smiled. "I know, but we can afford a dishwasher. Why do you insist on washing dishes by hand? I'll bet your fingers are like, totally wrinkled."

Although their kitchen contained all the modern conveniences, her gram preferred to clean dishes the old-fashioned way. "Never mind my fingers. I like to wash dishes. Sit down," she instructed with her back to her granddaughter. "I'll pour you some juice."

"Thanks, Nana. It's really hot outside." Through wide eyes, she glanced at her grandmother. "May I have some of that garlic bread?"

Hannah turned. She glanced at Madison with twinkling eyes, and then wiped her hands on her apron. "Not now, you'll spoil your appetite."

Since her Nana came to visit, every day was the same. Madison returned home from school, and Nana had cooked a hot meal or delectable treats. Likewise, Madison always asked to sample the delicacies. With unwavering regularity, her nana had always said, *"No. It'll spoil your dinner."*

The family matriarch retrieved a glass from the cabinet, and went to the refrigerator. As she poured Madison a glass of juice, she peered at the clock over the sink. "You're running a little late today aren't you?"

"Yes, Nana. Corric walked me home from the bus stop." Madison pulled a seat from beneath the table. "He doesn't go school." She sat, then scooted the chair up. "This is the third time he's walked me home this week. He's much older. Twenty-three, I think. That kinda creeps me out."

Nana set the cool glass on the table. The heat from the oven had already caused beads to form on the outside of the tumbler. Brow knit, Nana bit her lower lip. "An older guy, huh? Does this Corric seem to like you?"

Matty shrugged, then ran her fingers over the moist glass. "I don't know. Maybe." She tucked her foot beneath her, and lowered her gaze. Talking about guys with her nana always embarrassed her. Yet, Hannah had never judged her, so they discussed everything.

"It sounds to me like he's getting serious about you." Hannah placed her hand over her mouth. "He seems much too old for you. I trust there's nothing to this. Besides, what happened to Brice? He goes to your school." The twinkle in her eyes revealed her hidden grin.

A smile tugged at the corners of Madison's lips, too. Nothing pleased her more than the joy in her grandmother's countenance. Lifting the glass, she then sipped the juice. After she set the receptacle on the table, she rubbed her hands on her jeans several times. "Brice? Well, after Corric entered the scene, he kinda disappeared. Nana. Can I ask you a question?"

With an air of good humor, Hannah replied, "Sure, you can ask me anything, but I reserve the right not to answer." She snickered at her joke.

Once Nana returned to her duties at the sink, Madison found the courage to continue. "How *do* you know when a guy really likes you?"

Nana stopped washing dishes and turned to face her granddaughter. Resting her elbows against the sink, she appeared serious for the first time. "Sweetheart, that's a difficult question to answer. It's hard to know how somebody else really feels." Perspiration moistened the creases that formed on her temple. "Get to know that person well enough, and you'll have a good idea of when he's serious, and when he isn't."

"Well, some of the girls have been talking..." Madison paused, trying to decide if this was a discussion she wanted to have.

Frowning, Hannah pressed. "Talking about what?" Madison knew her Nana would continue to press until she got the information she wanted. "What are you trying to say?"

Madison cleared her throat. "Some of the girls have been saying that when you really like a guy, you...the two of you...well, that is...you have to show it."

Nana placed her dish towel on the counter. Her wavy locks fell into her face as she crossed the room. With the back of her damp hand, she swept the hair from eyes. The thick mane had hidden her stunning beauty. Madison examined the smooth skin of her grandmother's flawless face. It was difficult for her to believe she was over sixty years old. "Are you trying to ask me about sex?"

To avoid meeting her grandmother's gaze, Madison stared at the kitchen floor. "In a way, I guess I am."

Although Hannah appeared to relax, she scrutinized Madison's every gesture. After she pulled out a chair, she sat across from her grandchild. "Are you trying to tell me that you're thinking about having sex, Madison?"

When Hannah called her Madison, Matty realized the tone of the conversation had shifted from curiosity to solemnity. However, a desire from deep within pushed her forward. "No, Nana—not me," she insisted, "but some of the girls say the only way to prove to a guy that you really care, is to have sex with him. A few of the guys have said this too."

"Well, they're wrong. You didn't even mention love. You said cared about. I care about my plants, but I don't sleep with them. Just because you have feelings for someone doesn't mean you have sex with him."

As she leaned forward, Madison lifted her glass. "But Tisa says sex is the only way you can prove your love for a guy." She traced a capital "M" in the ring on the table. "You have to have sex, or he'll get it from someone else."

Hannah placed her hand atop Madison's then leaned inches from her. "Sweetheart, if a guy really cares about you, he won't push you into doing something you're not ready for. Preferably, he'll wait until after marriage. That's what love is all about — doing what's best for the other person."

Madison turned her head. "But isn't it true that a guy will lose interest in you, if you don't?"

After a deep sigh, Hannah massaged her ear. "Maybe, but you've got to respect yourself to demand respect from him. No man wants a relationship with a young woman who'll give herself to just anybody without a commitment. Besides, if he won't wait until you're ready, he's not worthy of you."

Swallowing hard, Madison forced a smiled. "I like that idea. He has to be worthy of me."

Relief washed over Hannah's face. "I know it's not popular for a girl to wait. But it's the right thing to do. There are no physical or mental consequences when you wait, honey. No matter how old he is, don't let anybody persuade you to do something you'll regret."

Embarrassed, Madison pulled out her phone, then lightly stroked the screen. "I thought I was ready, Nana. The other girls always tease me. They said Corric is not too old for me, and that I'm making a big deal over nothing."

Hannah smiled and lifted Madison's chin so that their eyes met. "There's a little voice in the back of your mind. When something's not right, it'll let you know. Follow the guidance of that little voice. It'll never steer you wrong."

"A voice in the back of my mind," Madison repeated. "I felt weird when Corric started meeting me at the bus stop. Is that what you mean?"

"It's called your conscience. You always know when something's wrong. Besides, you're only fourteen. There're many experiences ahead of you before you make a commitment like that. Don't be pressured into this experience by someone who is looking for an easy lay. Young girls are easily manipulated by an older man." She put her palm on Madison's cheek. "Take your time, sweetheart. Do this God's way. Once you make that step, you can't take it back."

~End~

CHAPTER THREE

Hurtful Lies

Countless young men and women have been sucked into the abyss of sexual immorality. Adults in whom adolescents place their confidence have violated that trust. Unfortunately, in today's society, too many children are growing up in homes without strong role models. In an effort to fill this emotional void, young people rely on older individuals who can manipulate their vulnerability. When an adult betrays the trust an adolescent places in him/her for sexual gratification, it is nothing less than abuse. So where do you turn to find the parent for whom you so desperately long? The answer is, of course, to Father God.

Young people may find themselves wondering why they should preserve their chastity when there seems to be someone who truly loves them. There are several reasons. First, your body is a temple, which deserves to be revered. You are so precious to Jesus, so very valuable, that he suffered and died to purchase your body with His blood. If someone loves you, he/she will not do anything that will dishonor you before God. When you have sex without the commitment of marriage, you are not only dishonoring your body, but you are also dishonoring your relationship with God.

CHAPTER FOUR

A PRECIOUS VESSEL

"Do you know that your body is a temple of the Holy Spirit, who is in you, whom you have received from God? you are not your own; you were bought at a price. Therefore, honor God with your body." (1 Cor.6:19-20 NIV).

In the Scriptures, sexual relations outside of marriage are compared to prostitution. This emphasizes how dangerous it is for two people to join without marriage.

Do you know that he who unites himself with a prostitute is one with her in body; for it is said, "The two will become one flesh. But he who unites himself with the Lord is one with him in spirit." (1 Cor. 6:15-17).

This analogy is fitting because fornication is a union that defiles the body. Is it any worse for a prostitute or a gigolo to sell his/her body than it is for us to give ourselves without commitment? The answer is a resounding no! Sex is a beautiful experience, but it is meant to be shared within the bonds of marriage. "Marriage is honorable among all, and the bed undefiled; but fornicators and adulterers God will judge." (Hebrews 13:4 NKJV).

Sex is referred to as consummating a relationship. What does this really mean? To consummate means to make perfect or to complete in every way. When two people marry, they are united spiritually, mentally, emotionally, and physically. Therefore, the ultimate goal of consummating a relationship is to perfect an existing bond. Marriage, a union instituted by God, is the only way to make love pure.

Therefore, a man shall leave his father and mother and be joined to his wife, and they shall become one flesh. "And they were naked, the man and his wife, and were not ashamed." (Genesis 2:24-25 NKJV).

If you are unmarried, there is only one bond that can sustain you, the love of Jesus. "Those who belong to Christ Jesus have crucified the flesh with its passions and desires." (Galatians 524 NIV). Rather than give your body to another person, you can give yourself to the Lord. He will fill every empty space in your heart. Those lustful desires that you thought you couldn't control will come under submission.

All other sins you commit are outside your body, separate and apart from you, *but he who sins sexually, sins against his own body.* (1 Cor. 6:18). The body is a temple that houses the Holy Spirit, and the Holy Spirit will not dwell in an unclean temple. You are a precious vessel whom God will fill with His perfect love. All you need to do to receive this love is ask, and it will be given to you. (Matt. 7:7).

CHAPTER FIVE

I'M SORRY GOD! PLEASE, LET ME START OVER.

A JEALOUS GOD

Although God is a loving Father, we can anger Him with our conduct and displease Him. God is a jealous God who refuses to take second place in our lives. When we place our desires before God, we relegate Him to second position, resulting in idolatry. The worship of idols, placing anything in your life above your relationship with God, simply is not permitted. Surely, no one wants to do anything that will evoke displeasure in God. Put to death, therefore, whatever belongs to your earthly nature: sexual immorality, impurity, lust, evil desires and greed, which is idolatry. Because of these, the wrath of Good is coming (Col. 3:5-5 NIV).

If we are to be obedient to God, we must live a pure life. His will for us is that we remain faithful to Him, by saving our bodies until we enter into marriage. Each of us is called to control his/her body in a way that is holy an honorable, not in passionate lust like the heathen, who do not know God. (1 Thessalonians 4:4-5 NIV).

No matter what we have done we can be forgiven. We are redeemed through the blood of Christ. Even the woman who was caught in the act of adultery was worthy of forgiveness. Recall, the Pharisees were demanding the stoning of this woman for her sins, but what did Jesus say? "If any one of you is without sin, let him be the first to throw a stone." (John 8:7 NIV). No one threw that stone. Like you and me, none of them was without sin. Although Jesus did not condemn her, He did not condone what she had done. Jesus declared, "Go now and leave your life of sin." (John 8:11 NIV). Jesus knows what we have done in our lives, and his instructions to us are the same as they were to this woman. "Go, and leave your life of sin."

**TKO!
I'VE GOT THE
POWER!**

CHAPTER SIX

FORGIVEN

Rahab, the prostitute in Jericho who hid the two spies, went on to be recognized as a woman of great faith. "By faith, the prostitute, Rahab, because she welcomed the spies, was not killed with those who were disobedient." (Hebrews 11:31 NIV). Rahab's story shows us that through faith, even a prostitute can be redeemed and raised to a higher level. Her descendants included Boaz, Obed, Jesse, David, Solomon, and Joseph; the husband of Mary, the mother of Jesus. Consider that, this is the same Jesus who died for our sins.

If Jesus can forgive the woman caught in the act of adultery, He will forgive you. To change your life, turn it over to the Lord. That's all you need to do. He can and will cleanse your body, your spirit, and your soul. There is nothing you have done that Jesus won't fix. Remember, Rahab went from prostitution to a position of honor among the faithful. Look to God to fill your heart. There is no greater father's love than the love of Father God.

~End~

Penelope A. Fields

ABOUT THE AUTHOR

Penelope A. Fields was born in East Texas, the last of five children, and the only daughter of Franklin and Johnnie Johnson. A quiet child, Penelope spent countless hours with her mother. Since she had no female siblings, her mother entertained her by reading to her, and instilling a passion that would last a lifetime.

Penelope attended Wiley College, where she graduated Summa Cum Laude. After receiving her Bachelor of Science degree in English, she went on to do graduate studies at the University of Texas at Tyler and Stephen F. Austin University. She received her elementary certification from East Texas Baptist University, and her Masters of Bible Studies from Warren Robbins University. Although she has worked as an independent beauty consultant and a lab technician, her greatest love is teaching English. Interacting with her seniors keeps her mind stimulated and keeps her challenged.

While she was a student in Waskom, Penelope met her high school sweetheart, LaVaughn. The couple married during her sophomore year in college. Her husband has been an inspiration to Penelope, encouraging and supporting her in every endeavor. Together, they have two wonderful adult children and one grandchild in whom they take great pride.

Email: pinelopa@earthlink.net

http://www.topazpublishingllc.com